Firs

The
Rainforest

Written by Chris Madsen
Illustrated by Andrew Locke

Woodbridge, England

The rainforest

A rainforest isn't just a place where trees grow - it **is** the trees. It's not just a forest where it rains, but a forest which **makes** rain.

Being inside the forest is a bit like being underwater. The wide tree tops - some as big as a football pitch - join together to make a roof hundreds of feet over your head. The sun is shining on the tree tops but it's dark on the floor far below, between their wide, smooth trunks. Other plants that live there have to climb up the trees to find some light for themselves.

The big trees are covered with other plants. Long, thin trees called **lianas** twist around the big tree-trunks and branches. Short, tufty plants like **pineapples** sit in the forks of trees, and there are pale, mysterious **orchids**, feathery **ferns** and trailing **mosses**.

Most of the animals of the forest are up there, too, where the food is. It's very noisy. Monkeys and bright birds chatter and scream, frogs croak, insects buzz, but the snakes just slither around silently. Everything has its special place, exactly as if they had their own special floor in a skyscraper. The trees are full of creatures trying hard not to slip and fall down onto the ground, far below.

In the tree tops

High up in the tree tops, it's sunny and warm. There are leaves and flowers and fruit to eat all year around, because there's no winter in the rainforest.

Leaf-eating monkeys called **langurs** live here. Leaf-eating lizards like **iguanas** also climb up to feed and sunbathe. Wherever there are leaves there are bound to be caterpillars, and the rainforest is full of glorious butterflies.

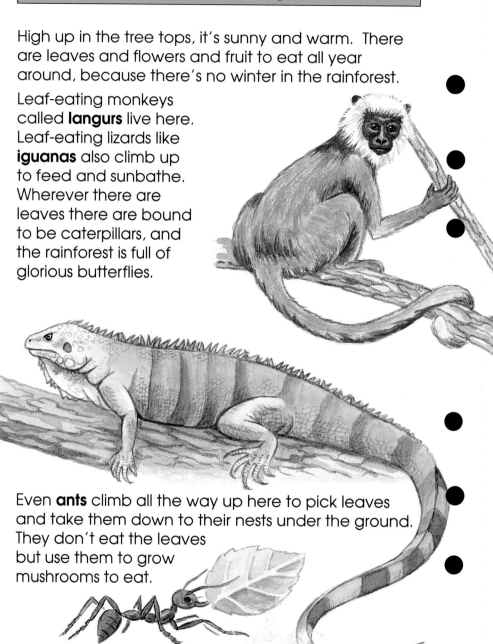

Even **ants** climb all the way up here to pick leaves and take them down to their nests under the ground. They don't eat the leaves but use them to grow mushrooms to eat.

There are **eagles** here, too, soaring above the canopy looking for birds and monkeys to eat.

There are wonderful fruits, too. **Parrots**, **hornbills** and **toucans** love to eat them, and so do **spider monkeys**. The **lipstick tree** makes bright red fruit to catch the eye of birds, and people who live in the forests use them for make-up.

Many of the animals which live in the tree tops never come down to the ground at all. If they did, they might not be able to climb back up the smooth tree-trunks.

Among the branches

Lower down, under the tree top canopy, the vines and lianas wind among the tree branches to make an endless climbing-frame. Everything that lives here has to be an expert climber, but they all do it in different ways.

Sloths go very slowly. They hang underneath branches, hooked on by their long, curved claws, patiently chewing leaves. Sloths are hardly ever the right way up. Even their fur grows from the middle of their tummy down to their back instead of the usual way round. Their back fur is lighter than their tummy fur, too, which is also the opposite of the way most animals' fur is coloured. Another strange thing about sloths is that their fur looks green. Tiny plants live right inside the hairs. This helps to make them hard to see among the leaves.

Monkeys already have four hands for climbing, which makes it a lot easier for them than it is for us. As well as these hands, **South American woolly monkeys** and **spider monkeys** also have a long tail for clinging onto branches, called a prehensile tail. With its tail wrapped tightly round a branch, a spider monkey can safely move its hands and feet without falling.

Nesting in trees

Living high up in the trees means having your babies there, too.

The forest is full of frogs. Most of them have little sticky pads on their feet for climbing instead of webs for swimming.

All frogs need water for their tadpoles, but the **rainforest tree frogs** find their water in very unusual places.

They lay their eggs in little puddles of rainwater that form in forked branches, or tree holes, or even in the hollow centres of pineapple plants. Here, the tadpoles feed on mosquito larvae - yes, they're here, too - until they turn into frogs and can go off hunting other insects among the branches and leaves.

Boa snakes don't lay eggs at all, like most other snakes do. The mother snake keeps her eggs inside her body until the babies hatch. This is much safer than leaving them on the ground.

There aren't enough tree-holes to go around. Any creature that is lucky enough to find one empty has to work very hard to keep it. The male **hornbill** keeps invaders out of his nest by sealing his mate in with mud before she lays her eggs. He feeds her while she's imprisoned, but he doesn't break the wall down to let her out until the babies are ready to fly.

On the ground

Down on the ground it's warm and damp. Everything that falls down from above - leaves, fruit, animal droppings - is gobbled up by the ants, giant millipedes, beetles and other creatures that swarm there. Nothing is wasted. Even fallen trees are eaten up by termites. On the forest floor, scavenging is a way of life.

There aren't many large animals down here, except for a few scavengers such as the wild pigs called **peccaries**, and strange **tapirs**. Some hunters prowl here, looking for prey, like the short-legged **bushdogs** of South America.

Because it's so dark, many forest plants and creatures are brightly coloured so that they can be seen. The biggest flower in the world, called Rafflesia, lives here. Rafflesias grow to 3 feet (1 metre) across; they're bright red and they smell of rotten meat to attract the flies which spread their pollen.

Making a noise is another way to attract attention in the dark, and this is the reason why rainforests are so noisy. **Howler monkeys** have a terrible roar, which sounds like a leopard. Every morning, the howling of **gibbons** mixes with birds and insects in the deafening dawn chorus.

People of the rainforests

People have lived in the rainforests for thousands and thousands of years. There weren't any shops to buy things, but they knew how to find everything they needed in the forest. There is lots of fruit and meat to eat, if you know how and where to find or catch it. There are medicines, too. A lot of the medicines we use come from rainforests, and the people who live there know about lots more besides.

Many forest people live near rivers, which give them water to drink and fish to eat. Rivers are good for travelling through the rainforest. Going on foot takes a long time, and it's easy to get lost. Going by boat is quicker and easier, and you can always be sure where you're going.

Making a boat is an important job. The people all work together to make a big canoe for the village. First, the right kind of tree has to be found and cut down. Then it is hollowed out and finally it is half-burned to make it strong and waterproof.

Another important job is hunting. A lot of rainforest people use arrows tipped with poison, because hunting is difficult in the dark, dense forest. The most famous arrow-poison of all comes from the skin of **South American frogs**, but most other arrow-poisons come from plants.

Fishes

The rainforests are packed with creatures that don't live anywhere else on Earth, and this includes fishes. Some of them, such as piranhas, are famous.

Piranhas aren't very big, but they have sharp teeth. They hunt in gangs that can strip all the meat off a 100lb wild pig in less than a minute.

The River Amazon also contains the most powerful electric fish in the world. It can give a shock more than twice as strong as the electricity supply in your home.

There are probably seven times as many different kinds of fish in the Amazon forest as there are in all of Europe. We don't know much about most of them, but there is one with jaws so strong that it can crack rubber-tree seeds harder than Brazil nuts.

Lots of Amazon fishes eat seeds and fruit. Each year, when the rivers flood, they go into the forest to stuff themselves.

Birds

Rainforests are full of brightly-coloured birds, from the big, noisy parrots and macaws to the tiny jewelled hummingbirds.

The name parrot includes **macaws, cockatoos, parakeets** and **lovebirds**. They all have strong beaks, which the bigger parrots use for climbing as well as eating. It isn't easy to fly around up there among the lianas, so rainforest parrots mostly clamber around like monkeys.

Macaws are parrots with beaks strong enough to crack nuts. They live in South America.

Toucan beaks are big and bright. Nobody knows the reason why their beaks are like this, because they eat quite soft fruit.

Hornbills also have a huge bill, but are not usually as brightly-coloured as toucans. They live in Asia and Africa, and toucans live in South America.

Hummingbirds dart everywhere in the rainforest, hunting for flowers. When they find one full of nectar they hover in front of it, sipping with their long beak. Their wings beat so quickly that they almost become invisible.

With so many animals prowling around in the trees, it can be dangerous setting up home to raise a family. One solution has been found by **oropendula** birds, which weave a nest like a raffia basket, hanging right at the tip of a branch.

Reptiles

In the rainforest rivers there are all kinds of **crocodiles**. Some have long thin snouts with very sharp teeth for fishing, and some hunt bigger prey.

Crocodiles hunt big land animals by waiting patiently until something comes to drink at the river. They float with just their back and nose and eyes out of the water, looking like old dead trees which have toppled in. When a small animal comes to drink, the crocodile opens its huge mouth and snaps it up. If the animal is a big one, the crocodile may just grab a leg and spin around very fast in the water until it twists right off. Then the crocodile can swallow it.

There are **turtles** in the rivers, too, and some swimming snakes. But most snakes live up in the trees. The most famous snakes of rainforests are the huge constrictors. They get their name from the way they kill their prey. When a **constrictor** finds something to eat, it wraps its coils around the prey and hugs it to death before it swallows it. Snakes don't eat very often, though, and spend a lot of their life curled up fast asleep.

Cats

Cats are good at climbing. They use their sharp claws to grip and their long tail to balance. It's not surprising that a lot of cats live in the rainforest.

Even the big cats can climb up trees. They use trees to keep their food safe from the scavengers on the ground. Leopards and jaguars are strong enough to pull a deer up into a tree, where they can feed in peace.

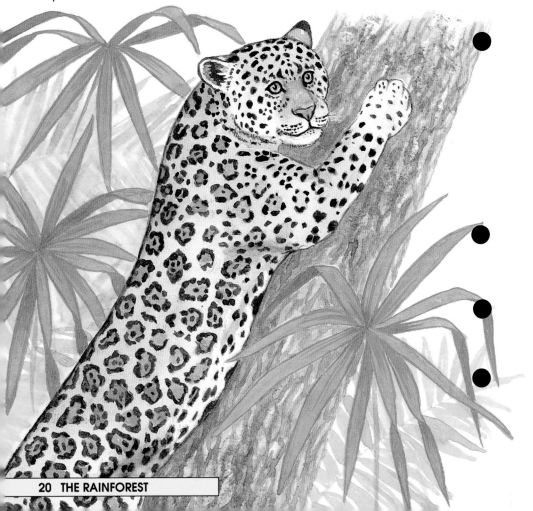

In Africa and Asia, the big forest cat is the **leopard**. **Black panthers** are leopards whose whole coat is black. They still have leopard spots, though. You can see them as shiny patches when the light catches a panther's coat in the right way.

Jaguars, which live in South America, have a shorter tail than leopards and their spots are bigger. They both have their spots arranged in a ring, or rosette, but the jaguar's rosette has a spot in the middle and the leopard's rosette is empty.

Smaller cats, such as **margay** and **ocelot**, also live deep in the forest. One of the strangest cats of all is the mysterious **jaguarundi**, which eats fruit as well as meat.

Monkeys

Monkeys have a tail, and apes do not. There are many different kinds of monkeys, but only a few apes. Gorillas, chimpanzees and orang-utans are apes, and so are gibbons.

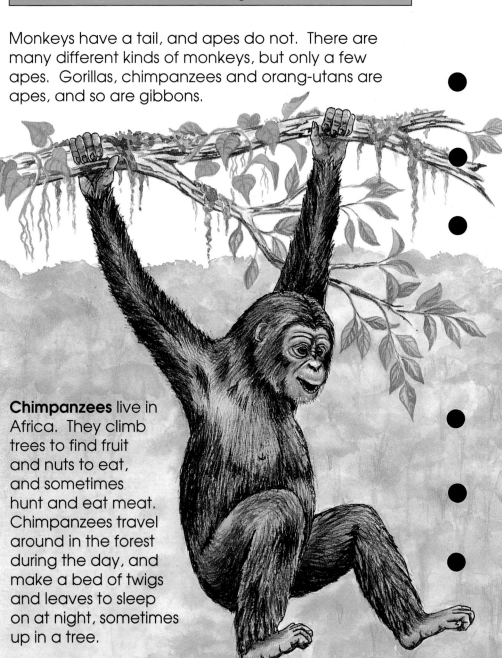

Chimpanzees live in Africa. They climb trees to find fruit and nuts to eat, and sometimes hunt and eat meat. Chimpanzees travel around in the forest during the day, and make a bed of twigs and leaves to sleep on at night, sometimes up in a tree.

Marmosets are monkeys which look a little like squirrels. They have silky hair, which sometimes makes a long mane around their neck and head. They eat insects as well as fruit and buds, and have high twittery voices.

The strange **uakaris** live high in the treetops and hardly ever come down. They are very shy monkeys, and blush easily when they're upset.

Another monkey with a colourful face is the **mandrill**, which lives in Africa. It has a long face like a dog, with some very big teeth, too. Mandrills live mostly on the ground, where they eat a lot of insects, and their tails are quite short.

Africa and Madagascar

Gorillas live deep in African forests. They grow to about the same height as a person, but are much broader and heavier. Although a big gorilla can look very frightening, they are very quiet and shy and only eat fruit and leaves.

The biggest frog in the world lives in Africa. The **goliath frog** grows to more than a foot (30 cm) long. It lives in deep river pools in the rainforest.

African constrictor snakes are called **pythons**, and they can grow to more than 20 feet (6 metres) long. Snakes can't chew, so they swallow their prey whole. A big African python can swallow a whole pig.

Okapis are nearly as big as horses, but they are very shy and only move about at night. People hardly ever see them when they creep down to the riverbank to feed on the plants there.

At the side of Africa is a very big island called Madagascar. The animals here are very different from African ones. Instead of monkeys, there are **lemurs**. They have clever hands and long tails, too.

South America

South America has the biggest rainforest in the world, a very watery place full of huge rivers. Some wonderful animals live in the Amazon rivers.

In the dark, deep forest, the banks of a river are a place where the sun can get in to make plants grow. A lot of animals live by the water, and some live right in it.

Manatees are big, lazy creatures. They float in the water in herds, grazing on waterweeds.

The Amazon river is so big that it even has its own small whales. Amazon river dolphins, called **botos**, have a long, thin nose for catching fish.

Giant otters grow as long as a person, if you include the tail. They're very curious, and make a lot of noise as they play in the water, deep in the forest. They are now very rare, because people hunt them for their fur.

Turtles are hunted, too, for their shells, their meat, and their eggs. **River turtles** come every year in great gangs to lay their eggs on muddy islands in the middle of the river.

Asia

The forests of Asia also have their special animals.

The name of the **orang-utan** means 'old man of the woods'. Like most apes, orang-utans are shy, peaceful creatures. They are not as tall as gorillas, and much thinner, and their arms are a lot longer than their legs. Orang-utans move around slowly in the forest, swinging by their arms and sometimes walking on the ground. At night, each member of the family makes a stick nest to sleep in, up in a tree. Their favourite food is durian fruit.

The flowers of the durian tree are pollinated by bats. **Durian fruit** has a very strange smell, but some people like eating it as much as orang-utans do.

Another shy creature is the **slow loris**. As its name says, it moves very slowly when it creeps around at night, hunting small sleeping birds, lizards and insects. Its big eyes help it to see in the dark.

The most famous Asian forest beast is the **tiger**. The tiger's stripes help it to hide in the forest. It's hard to see a dozing tiger during the day, and even harder to see one when it comes out to hunt at night. Tigers hunt alone, creeping up on their prey in the forest and then pouncing quickly. Tigers don't like to be too hot, and often lie in a river to keep cool.

Australia

In the dense rainforests of Australia and New Guinea, some kangaroos and wallabies have learnt to climb trees to find food or escape from danger.

One creature which never comes down to the ground is the **flying phalanger**. This little animal can glide from one tree to another, by stretching two flaps of furry skin between its front and back legs. It has a pouch with room for two babies, but they very soon come out to cling to their mother's fur. Perhaps it's safer on top.

The **spotted cuscus** is less daring. It creeps about slowly, hanging on tightly with all four feet and a prehensile tail, too. Although it looks a bit like the loris on page 29, it's really a marsupial with a pouch.

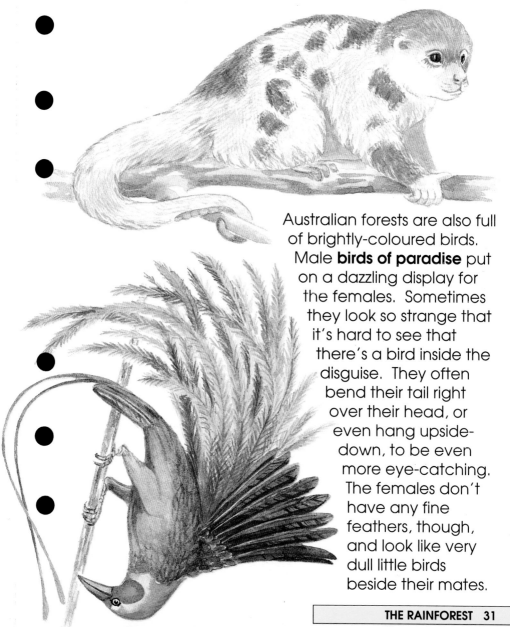

Australian forests are also full of brightly-coloured birds. Male **birds of paradise** put on a dazzling display for the females. Sometimes they look so strange that it's hard to see that there's a bird inside the disguise. They often bend their tail right over their head, or even hang upside-down, to be even more eye-catching. The females don't have any fine feathers, though, and look like very dull little birds beside their mates.

What rainforests give us

Rainforests give the world plants.
Rainforests contain more than three-quarters of all the plants in the world.

A patch of rainforest can have 250 different kinds of trees in the same space where ordinary forests only have 25.

Rainforests give the world food.
Some of the foods which have come from rainforests are: aubergines; avocados; bananas; Brazil-nuts; capsicums; chocolate; cucumber; guava; mango; melons; papaya; passion fruit; sweet potatoes; tapioca

Rainforests give the world medicines.
One quarter of all our medicines have come from rainforest plants. This includes quinine for malaria; anti-cancer drugs (3/4 of our anti-cancer drugs come from rainforest plants); plus things which go into cough medicines and others that go on your toes when you get chilblains.

Rainforests give the world hot and cold drinks.
Coffee, cocoa and Cola drinks all came from the rainforests.

Rainforests give the world flavour
Pepper and vanilla come from the rainforests, too... ...and rubber bands.

Rainforests give the world oxygen.
All those trees (three-quarters of the land plants in the whole world, remember) help to make the world's air good for us and other animals to breathe.